HUNT!
Can You Survive the Stone Age?

By Julia Bruce
Illustrated by Peter Dennis

Enslow Elementary

an imprint of

 Enslow Publishers, Inc.
40 Industrial Road
Box 398
Berkeley Heights, NJ 07922
USA

http://www.enslow.com

Enslow Elementary, an imprint of Enslow Publishers, Inc.
Enslow Elementary® is a registered trademark of Enslow Publishers, Inc.

US edition published in 2009 by Enslow Publishers, Inc.
First published in 2007 by Orpheus Books Ltd.,
6 Church Green, Witney, Oxfordshire, OX28 4AW, England

Copyright ©2009 Orpheus Books Ltd.

Created and produced by
Julia Bruce, Rachel Coombs, Nicholas Harris, Sarah Hartley, and Erica Simms, Orpheus Books Ltd.
Text Julia Bruce
Illustrated by Peter Dennis *(Linda Rogers Associates)*
Consultant Dr Christophe Soligo, Department of Anthropology, University College London

Library of Congress Cataloging-in-Publication Data
Bruce, Julia.
    Hunt! : can you survive the stone age? / Julia Bruce.
        p. cm. — (Step into history)
    Summary: "Learn how to survive an Ice Age winter" — Provided by publisher.
    Includes bibliographical references and index.
    ISBN-13: 978-0-7660-3476-1
    ISBN-10: 0-7660-3476-3
    1. Stone age—Juvenile literature. 2. Hunting—Juvenile literature. 3. Woolly mammoth—Juvenile literature. I. Title
GN768.B78 2009
930.1'2—dc22
                                        2008019761

To Our Readers: We have done our best to make sure all Internet Addresses in this book were active and appropriate when we went to press. However, the author and the publisher have no control over and assume no liability for the material available on those Internet sites or on other Web sites they may link to. Any comments or suggestions can be sent by e-mail to comments@enslow.com or to the address on the back cover.

Printed and bound in China.

10 9 8 7 6 5 4 3 2 1

Contents

The Challenge

IT IS 20,000 BC and Earth is in the grip of a bitter ice age. Massive ice sheets cover much of northern Europe, Asia, and North America. You are the chief of a small clan of humans that lives on the tundra. This is a frozen region of dry grassland that lies between the ice sheets in the north, and forest in the south. Only mosses, lichens, grasses, and low-lying shrubs can grow on this windswept land.

Life is hard here, but you and the clan have good ways of adapting, or changing to survive the harsh conditions. Men, women, and children all help the clan get enough food and supplies to survive. Men and boys hunt large mammals. Women and smaller children gather food from the forests and grasslands. It's not all hard work, though. Some in the clan will make cave paintings, small statues, musical instruments, and even toys.

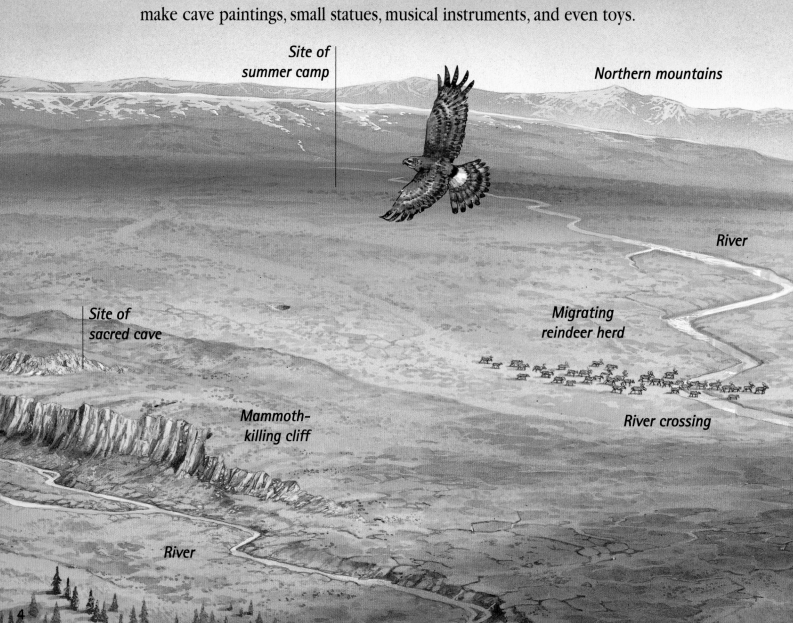

Site of
summer camp

Northern mountains

River

Site of
sacred cave

Migrating
reindeer herd

Mammoth-
killing cliff

River crossing

River

4

Winter is approaching. Your clan relies on the great herds of reindeer that roam the area. Their meat is your main food, and your clothes and shelters are made from their thick, warm hides. Their antlers and bones make good tools and weapons. But the lichens and grasses that the reindeer eat will soon be covered by snow. So they are moving south to the forest to find food. To survive, you must follow them on their migration.

How can you find safe campsites and keep warm at night? How do you make good tools and weapons? What's the best way to hunt and kill large mammals like the woolly mammoth? Find out as this guide takes you step-by-step through basic survival and hunting skills. Can you lead your clan on this dangerous journey—and bring them safely back to your camp on the tundra when the reindeer return in summer?

T U N D R A

Lake

Migrating woolly mammoths

Winter camp

Edge of the southern forest

On the Trail

The clan must be ready for this long and dangerous journey. Clothes and boots should be warm and well made. Carry basic tools, weapons for hunting and defense, and camping and fire-making equipment. Don't forget to bring extra food in case hunting is poor. Have a good hunter stay near the back of the group to help make sure no one falls behind.

Hunter warrior

Shaman

The chief's son

The clan chief

Clan members ready to set out on their journey

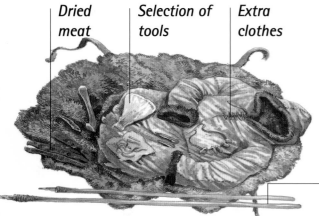

Dried meat

Selection of tools

Extra clothes

Spears

A traveling bundle

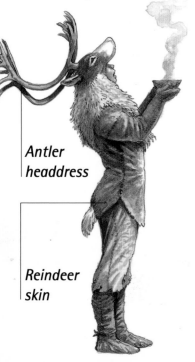

Antler headdress

Reindeer skin

The shaman is an important member of your clan. Your people believe that the land and animals all have spirits. They also believe that you talk with these spirits through your shaman. He wears reindeer antlers and skin to make him stand out.

Baby carrier

Walking stick

A backpack cradle makes it easy to carry babies and small children on the long journey. It is made from animal hide and lined with fur to keep the baby warm. It also leaves the carrier's hands free for other things, such as bags and a walking stick.

You will see many animals on your journey. Some will be good for food, such as fish, ducks, lemmings, and hares. Look for good places to hunt, fish, and trap these animals as you travel to keep a good supply of fresh food. Other animals are dangerous. For example, a woolly rhino can kill a person easily. Also beware of packs of wolves and cave lions.

Eider duck

Lemming

Salmon: can be caught with a harpoon

Hare: can be caught in a trap

Wolf: dangerous and clever hunter

Reindeer: an important source of food and materials such as bone, antler, and hide

Woolly rhinoceros: can be dangerous if provoked

Megaloceros: just one of these large deer would provide enough meat to feed the whole clan for a few days

Woolly mammoth: the largest animal on the tundra

Cave lion: will steal the animals you kill if it can

Keeping Warm

Fire is the most important resource on the journey. It will give warmth, cook food, and provide protection from wild animals. Find some flint (a kind of stone) and iron pyrite (a kind of metal ore). These create a spark when banged together. The best tinder, which is fine, dry material to catch the spark, is a type of fungus that grows only on trees. Collect this while the group is still in the southern forest and dry it out. Alternatively, dried grass can be used. A shell and a piece of leather will also help protect against flying sparks.

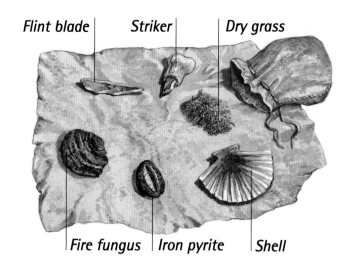

Flint blade | Striker | Dry grass

Fire fungus | Iron pyrite | Shell

SAFETY NOTE: FIRE IS VERY DANGEROUS. DO NOT TRY TO BUILD A FIRE YOURSELF WITHOUT AN ADULT TO HELP YOU.

1. Shavings from the dried fungus are scraped into the shell using the flint blade.

2. When banged together, the flint striker and iron pyrite create sparks.

3. More tinder can be used to light the fire from the small flame.

To make a fire, first build the fuel up in a rough cone shape. There are no trees on the tundra, so use low-growing shrubs or animal fat and bones as fuel. Dry material at the base of the cone helps it light the fuel. This is called kindling. Light the kindling using the dried tinder, such as fire fungus. Then feed the flame with more tinder. Fan the flames until the fire grows.

Fish will cook quickly over a hot, low-burning fire.

Use your fire to cook food on a spit. Skewer a piece of meat on a sharp stick and hold it over the heat. Keep turning it until it is cooked. Hot embers, or glowing pieces of wood, are good for roasting. Once you have the fire going, scrape some of the red-hot embers to one side. Set up your spit above this. The embers will give off an even heat for a long time, but they will not burn the food.

Spit | Hot embers scraped away from the main fire

Main fire

Cooking on a spit

Shallow pit

1. Dig a shallow pit and set a fire within it.

Stones

Hot embers

2. Place a layer of stones on the hot embers.

You can use a pit cooking method if the ground is not frozen. You must be able to dig into the earth. This method works well if you are busy during the day. Set it up in the morning. The food cooks all day and will be ready by evening.

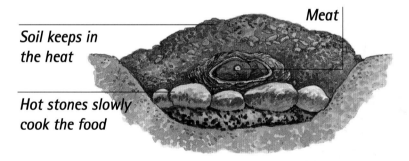

Soil keeps in the heat

Meat

Hot stones slowly cook the food

3. Place meat, wrapped in leather or leaves, on the stones and cover with soil. Leave for several hours.

A good cooking fire should be allowed to burn low and hot. You don't want lots of high flames as these will scorch the outside of the food before the inside is cooked.

Place large stones around the base of the fire. This will help contain the fire. The stones will also heat up. They will keep giving off heat even when the fire has died down.

To keep the fire burning overnight for warmth and safety from wild animals, add a layer of slow-burning fuel.

Tools and Weapons

Good tools and weapons are essential for survival. Make sure you have a supply of raw materials to make new tools if you need to. Hard, smooth stone, such as flint, is best for sharp knives and spears. Bone and antlers are also good for making tools. You will need wood and animal gut, or strips of hide, to make harpoons and spears. It is important to have skilled tool makers with you on the hunt.

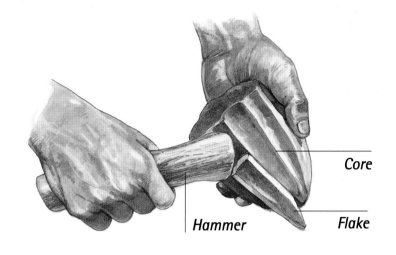

Core

Hammer

Flake

To make sharp tools like knives, start with a flint core. This is a stone that has already been shaped. Use an antler hammer to knock a flake off the core.

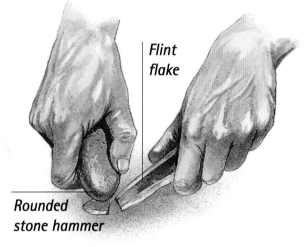

Flint flake

Rounded stone hammer

Snap off the end of the flake to give it a flat edge. A rounded stone is good for this job.

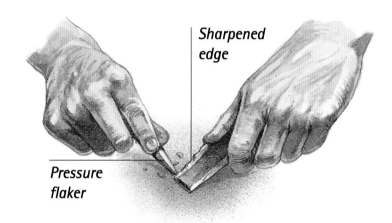

Sharpened edge

Pressure flaker

For a sharp blade, use pressure from an antler tool to flake off layers along the edge.

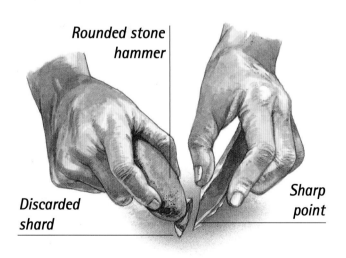

Rounded stone hammer

Discarded shard

Sharp point

To make a burin, a tool used for poking holes, strike the end of the flake at an angle. This makes the burin's sharp, triangular point.

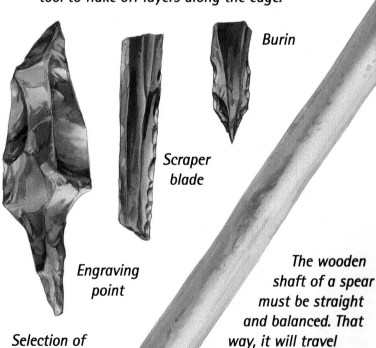

Burin

Scraper blade

Engraving point

Selection of flint tools

The wooden shaft of a spear must be straight and balanced. That way, it will travel straight when thrown.

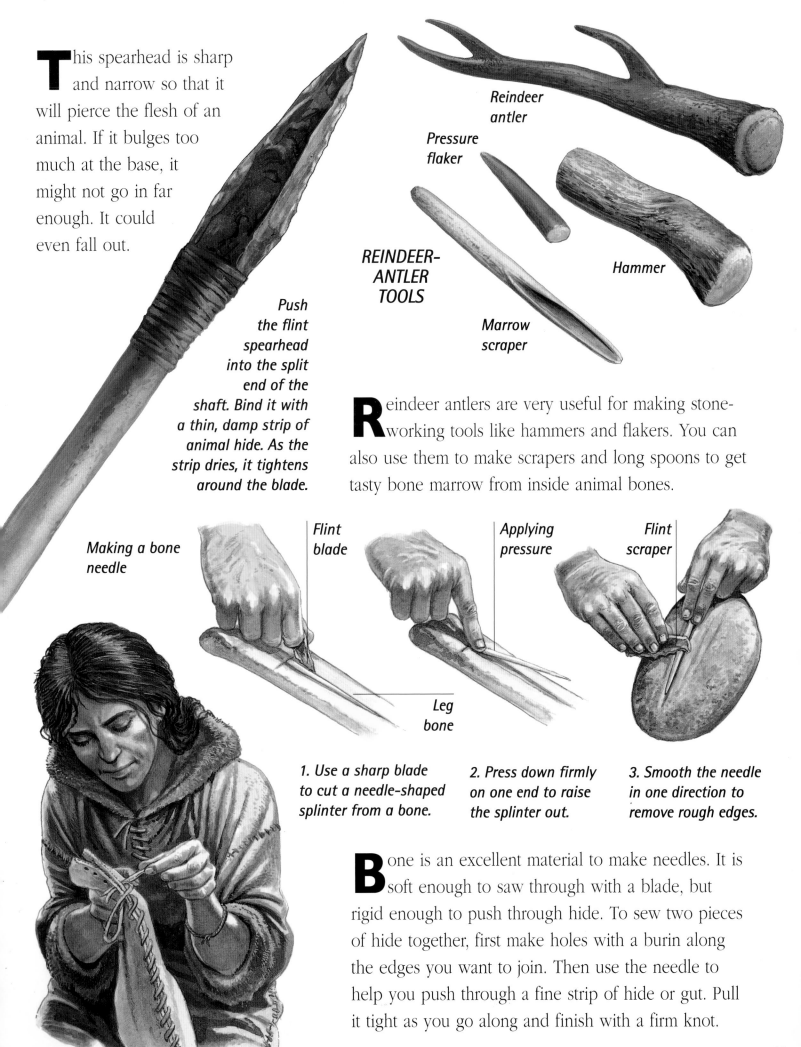

This spearhead is sharp and narrow so that it will pierce the flesh of an animal. If it bulges too much at the base, it might not go in far enough. It could even fall out.

Push the flint spearhead into the split end of the shaft. Bind it with a thin, damp strip of animal hide. As the strip dries, it tightens around the blade.

Reindeer antler

Pressure flaker

REINDEER-ANTLER TOOLS

Hammer

Marrow scraper

Reindeer antlers are very useful for making stone-working tools like hammers and flakers. You can also use them to make scrapers and long spoons to get tasty bone marrow from inside animal bones.

Making a bone needle

Flint blade

Applying pressure

Flint scraper

Leg bone

1. Use a sharp blade to cut a needle-shaped splinter from a bone.

2. Press down firmly on one end to raise the splinter out.

3. Smooth the needle in one direction to remove rough edges.

Bone is an excellent material to make needles. It is soft enough to saw through with a blade, but rigid enough to push through hide. To sew two pieces of hide together, first make holes with a burin along the edges you want to join. Then use the needle to help you push through a fine strip of hide or gut. Pull it tight as you go along and finish with a firm knot.

Finding Food

To survive on your long journey, you need to spend a large part of each day finding food. Food is scarce on the tundra, but there are some things to eat if you know how to find them. Everyone can be involved. You and the other hunters can hunt and trap animals, birds, and fish. Other members of the group can gather berries, fungi, eggs, shellfish, roots, and seeds.

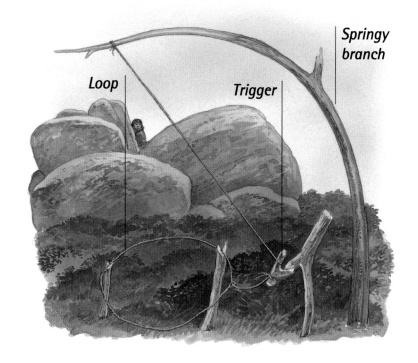

Loop   **Trigger**   **Springy branch**

Taking aim   **Fishing spear**   **Speared fish**

Trapping is an easy way to catch small animals and birds. Set traps overnight and check them in the morning. For a simple trap, make a loop with a slip knot from twisted grass. Set it where you see signs of animals, such as tracks, dung (animal waste), or flattened grass. Push a springy branch into the ground. Attach the snare and a trigger to it as shown above. An animal passing through the snare will move it and spring the trigger. The branch will spring upward and tighten the loop around the prey.

Fish are a very good source of food if you can catch them. Spearing them is tricky, but you can get lucky if you choose your spot carefully. Fish naturally gather where the river narrows. Fish also like places where the water gushes over boulders. Be careful not to cast your shadow onto the water when you take aim. The fish will see it and know you are there!

Throwing a spear

Digging for roots | Gathering berries

The women of your clan should be skilled in finding food from the land. In late summer and autumn there are berries, seeds, and mushrooms. Remember that some tundra birds lay their eggs on the ground. Look out for their nests and gather the eggs. Freshwater shellfish from rivers and streams are also a good source of food. Don't forget that food can be found underground, too. Some plant roots are good to eat. Never, ever eat unfamiliar fruit, mushrooms, or other plants because they might be poisonous.

Reindeer are your main source of meat and fur, antlers, and bone. You can hunt them as you follow the herd south on their migration, a seasonal journey to find food and warmer weather.

You and the other hunters should work together in a group. One part of the group tries to separate a few animals from the main herd. Then they drive these reindeer toward the rest of the hunters, who will be waiting with their spears ready to take a shot. One or two good shots should kill the reindeer.

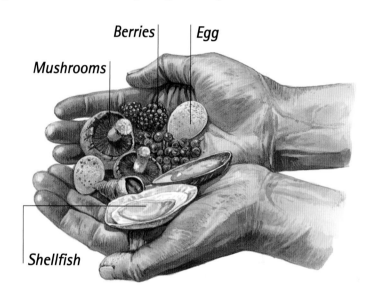

Mushrooms | Berries | Egg

Shellfish

Driving the reindeer toward the hunters

Making Camp

Sometimes you will be able to find shelter in caves or forests on your journey. But most of the time you will need to set up the tents and tepees that you carry with you on the journey. Set up your camp when you reach the reindeers' wintering ground at the edge of the forest. You can stay there for at least several weeks.

Frame poles | Tying poles together | Unloading hides | Setting up the frame

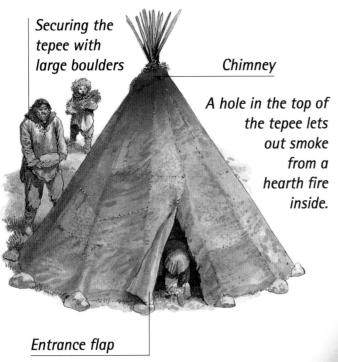

Securing the tepee with large boulders

Chimney

A hole in the top of the tepee lets out smoke from a hearth fire inside.

Entrance flap

Tepees can be put up and taken down again quickly. First lay the supporting poles on the ground. Tie them together near one end. Then lift up the poles and spread them out into a cone-shaped frame. Stretch sewn animal hides over the frame. Secure the whole structure with large rocks around the base.

While some of the clan are busy setting up camp, send others to scout around in search of food. If you are lucky, they could come across a group of migrating woolly mammoths. These huge animals also move south during the winter months looking for food. The animals at the back of the group are often the oldest and weakest of the herd. They have long tusks and walk more slowly.

Mammoths move in groups made of females and young. An older female, called the matriarch (MAY-tree-ark), leads the herd. She will do her best to make sure the animals in her herd are safe. She can even use her trunk to pull this young mammoth out of a freezing bog.

Mammoths are the largest animals on the tundra. They are normally too big for you to hunt and kill. But if they happen to stray close to a cliff edge, you have a good chance of running them off the cliff. Follow the herd with your best hunters as the animals approach the cliff. Try to separate the old females from the rest of the herd. Then drive them toward the edge with fire and your spears.

Many of your hunters will remember thrilling tales of mammoth hunts told to them as children around a fire.

Stragglers at the back of the group include three old females and a very young calf.

15

Don't underestimate your prey. Mammoths can use their tusks to toss attackers into the air if they get too close.

You and your hunters are in a lucky position with the herd traveling so close to a cliff edge. But there are other ways to kill mammoths. In areas where the ground is soft enough, you can dig a pit and trap your prey in it. Find a place where the animal often passes by. Disguise the pit by covering it with branches and leaves.

Throwing spears at a mammoth will not kill it, but it will help to drive it backward.

Mammoth Hunt

You have separated the three older mammoths who were lagging behind the rest of the group. You and the hunters have forced them toward the edge of the cliff with spears and torches. Now surround the animals. Push them closer and closer to the edge by prodding them with fire and throwing spears at them. Eventually, one beast will step back too far and stumble over the edge. Remember that you only need one to fall over. You can let the rest escape.

This mammoth is trapped between your hunters and the cliff edge.

Keep a lookout as the animals come close. If they look like they might pass by your trap, rush toward them in a group while shouting. Use spears and fire to drive them in the direction you need. Once one falls into the pit, it will be unable to climb out. You can then kill it quickly with spears and knives.

After the Hunt

If the hunt was successful, you will now have to carve the mammoth meat for food. A big, freshly killed mammoth will provide a large amount of food and other useful materials.

But it won't be long before other creatures discover your kill and try to take it from you. You must work fast. Get some of your men to butcher the mammoth. You can use all parts of the mammoth's body in some way. Order some of the hunters to build a fire and keep watch for prowling lions and wolves.

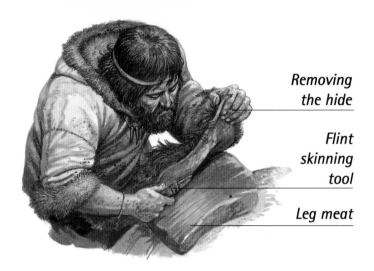

Removing the hide

Flint skinning tool

Leg meat

Skin the hide from smaller pieces of flesh like the legs. The meat will stay fresh for a week or two. You can smoke or dry it to preserve it and make it last longer. The small pieces of hide can be patched together for clothes or blankets.

Starting to skin the kill

Cliff

This mammoth has large tusks. You can remove them and use them as carrying poles for the meat and hide.

Throwing spears

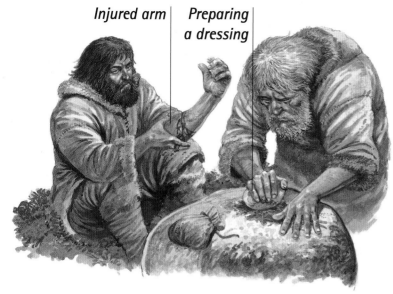

Injured arm | *Preparing a dressing*

Even on a successful hunt there may be a price to pay. Injuries are common when you hunt dangerous animals like mammoths or lions. You must make sure that you have someone skilled at healing injuries in your group. This person should keep a pouch of medicinal herbs and treat any injuries as soon as possible. Even with treatment, be aware that an injured hunter might still die.

Death is part of the struggle for survival on the tundra. Your hunters risk their lives when they tackle large prey. A flick of a mammoth tusk can kill a person. If you lose any of your people on your journey, you must give them a funeral. Your people believe this helps the person's spirit be at peace. Dig a grave as best you can in the frozen earth. If you cannot, cover the body with rocks. Follow your funeral rituals and bid farewell to your brave companion.

Funeral ritual

Shoulder-blade spade

Cave lions

Finding food in the winter is hard for all the animals of the tundra, even big, ferocious cave lions. They can smell a dead or dying animal, like your mammoth, from far away. They attack mostly at night, but they will come out in the day if they are hungry enough. Making noise and waving fiery torches or spears will scare them away. But don't lower your guard. They might come back and catch you by surprise.

Sacred Cave

After such a good hunt, you might want to visit the clan's sacred cave. For generations your people have come to this place, carved deep into the rock by an ancient river. Here they have recorded things about their world in paintings on the walls. While the artists are at work, the shaman dances to pipe music to celebrate the success of your mammoth hunt. This is also where your people remember the spirits of those you have lost.

Natural stones and minerals, such as red iron oxide (hematite) and black manganese dioxide, are used to make pigments, or colors for painting.

The minerals are ground into powder and mixed with water or animal fat in oyster-shell palettes.

Fine detail can be painted using fingers, sticks, or brushes made out of bone or wood and animal hair.

Patches of reindeer hide dipped in the pigment are used to color larger areas.

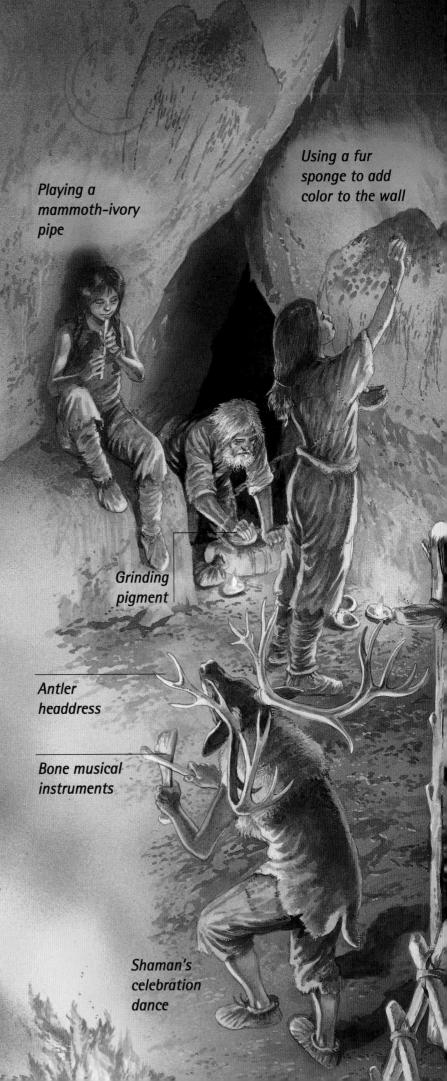

Playing a mammoth-ivory pipe

Using a fur sponge to add color to the wall

Grinding pigment

Antler headdress

Bone musical instruments

Shaman's celebration dance

Drawing a
Megaloceros
with a hair and
bone brush

Flames provide
just enough light
to work by.

Blowing pigment
directly on to the
cave wall leaves an
imprint of the
artist's hand

Hide, Tusk, and Bone

When you reach your winter camp you can start using some of the raw materials you got from the mammoth kill. Its meat already gave you food. Its fat is a good fuel. You will be at your winter camp for several weeks, so you will also have time to make clothing and tools from the mammoth's fur, hide, bones, and ivory. You can also catch other, smaller animals.

Smashing bones to get the marrow inside | *Cutting meat into strips for drying*

Even the bones of the mammoth can be a source of food. If you smash them with a stone hammer you can get to the tasty marrow inside. Cut some of the meat from the kill into strips and dry it out in the air or over a fire. Dried meat will keep for a long time and be light and easy to carry when you break camp. The children in your camp will do much of this work.

Scraping the hide | *Pegging hide to the ground*

Hides from animals such as reindeer and mammoth are a vital resource, but they need to be properly prepared. First they should be pegged out, fur side down, and stretched taut. Any remaining flesh should be removed with sharp flint scrapers. Then leave the hides to dry. They can be softened by rubbing in animal fat. Hides can be used whole or cut into pieces for sewing together warm clothes and boots.

Making sewing holes in hide | *Sewing boots together*

Mammoth bone and ivory can be made into many useful objects. They are perfect materials for carving beautiful ornaments, too. You can create beads, toys, and figures. Bone toys made into animal shapes make good toys for small children. Use flint tools to carve your figures and animal hide to polish them.

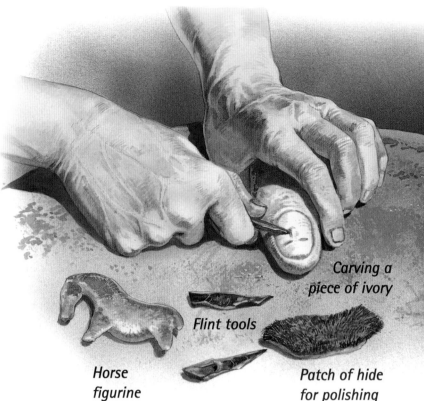

Carving a piece of ivory

Flint tools

Horse figurine

Patch of hide for polishing

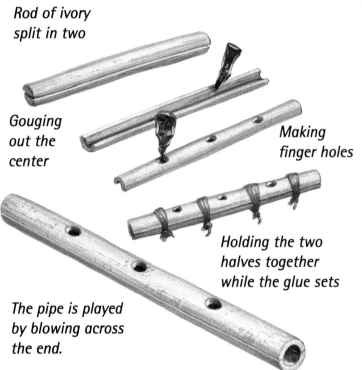

Rod of ivory split in two

Gouging out the center

Making finger holes

Holding the two halves together while the glue sets

The pipe is played by blowing across the end.

Bone and ivory are both good materials for making musical pipes. Ivory pipes make a very pure sound. Carve a piece of ivory as straight as you can. Then saw it in half and gouge out the middle. Pierce out some finger holes. Then stick the two halves back together with tree-sap glue.

Mammoth tusks and bones can be used to build strong shelters. The huts in your summer camp should be made this way. Tusks make a good frame. You can build up the walls with the huge thigh and jaw bones. You need the bones of many animals to do this. These can be scavenged from other mammoth skeletons on the tundra. Cover the tusk and bone framework with tough mammoth hides to make a nice hut.

Collecting bones   *Tying tusks together*   *Tusk supported in skull*

Summer Camp

Once the weather begins to warm up, the reindeer and mammoths will begin to head north again. You and the clan must go, too, because you depend on these animals for survival.

When it's time to break camp, be sure to pack the dried meat and sturdy new boots you have made. Everyone, including the children, must help get ready for the return journey north to the summer camp.

Glacier

Repairing a mammoth-bone hut

Making spears

Mammoth jaw bones

Learning to throw a spear

Mammoths

Returning
hunters

Rocks to weigh
down the
animal-hide roof

Hide
drying

When you arrive back at the site of your summer camp on the tundra, you must get the clan back into their summer routine: making weapons, preparing food, drying skins and meat.

One of the first things to do is to repair your huts. The animal-hide roofs will be damaged from winter storms. Keep a lookout for wolves and lions, especially at night. There is much work to do. But at least you can camp in one place for the summer months.

Animal-hide
roof

Mammoth
thigh bones

Preparing
fish to eat

Timeline

6 million years ago

The earliest known human ancestors live in Africa.

4.5 million years ago

Human ancestors are able to walk upright for some of the time. They are not yet modern humans. They are called hominids.

3.7 million years ago

Hominids called *Australopithecus afarensis* live in Ethiopia, Africa. Scientists have found their bones and fossilized footprints.

2.5 million years ago

Homo habilis, the first known true humans, evolve in Africa. Their name means "handy man." They use very simple stone tools. This is the beginning of the "Old Stone Age" or Paleolithic Age.

Antler hammer and stone hand axe made by **Homo heidelbergensis.**

2 million years ago

Homo erectus evolves in Africa, probably from *Homo habilis.* These humans are thought to be the ancestors of all later humans. They walk upright and are like modern humans, but their brains are a little smaller. They make about 12 different types of stone tools.

1.8 million years ago

The earliest known humans living outside Africa. Human fossils have been found on the borders of Europe and Asia.

1.6 million years ago

Homo erectus spread east into China and into Southeast Asia. They probably travel in search of new hunting grounds.

800,000 years ago

A new kind of human called *Homo heidelbergensis* evolves from *Homo erectus* and lives in Europe. The weather conditions there are very warm. They make tools from animal bone, antlers, and stone. They are expert hunters and have begun to use fire.

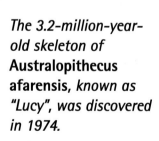

The 3.2-million-year-old skeleton of **Australopithecus afarensis,** *known as "Lucy", was discovered in 1974.*

480,000 years ago

The beginning of a very long cold period called a glacial stage. This will last 60,000 years. The ice cap at the North Pole spreads until it covers much of northern Europe, Asia, and North America. Humans have to learn how to survive in these new, colder conditions.

Neanderthal hunters lay a trap for a woolly mammoth.

300,000 years ago

In Europe, Neanderthals have evolved from *Homo heidelbergensis.*

270,000 years ago

The world's climate cools once again and Neanderthals adapt well to life in the cold. They have stocky bodies that help them conserve heat and large noses that warm the cold air as they breathe. They are good hunters. They use about 60 different stone tools. They also wear simple clothes made from animal skins to keep themselves warm.

200,000 years ago

Homo sapiens (modern humans) evolve from *Homo erectus* in East Africa.

120,000 years ago

The climate has warmed up again. Modern humans move into the Middle East from Africa.

A selection of Neanderthal tools.

60,000 years ago

After a long period of warmer weather, the world's climate cools down once more.

60–50,000 years ago

Modern humans reach Indonesia and then Australia. They use boats to "island hop" across the ocean.

Possible routes taken by modern humans from Africa though the Middle East, Asia, Indonesia, and into Australia.

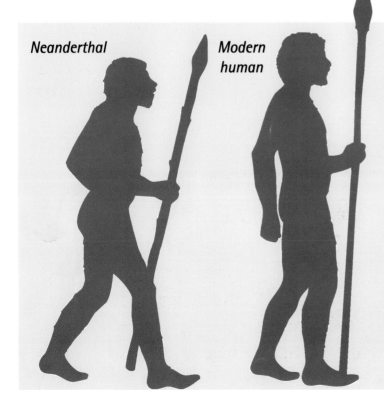

Neanderthal

Modern human

Modern humans and Neanderthals

Modern humans lived alongside Neanderthals in Europe for about 10,000 years. Modern humans were taller than Neanderthals. They looked very much like people do today.

Neanderthals were shorter and stockier with a heavier brow and larger jaw. Neanderthals' brains were slightly bigger than those of modern humans. However, modern humans still proved to be better hunters. They also made better tools and clothes and developed a much more complex language.

Timeline (continued)

35,000 years ago, modern humans have begun painting on cave walls.

38,000 years ago

The first modern humans from Africa have arrived in Europe. They adapt well to the cold. Over time they start competing for hunting and shelter with the Neanderthals.

35,000 years ago

Modern humans in Europe have begun expressing themselves with art. They produce cave paintings of themselves and the animals they hunt. They also make beads and carvings of human and animal figures in bone, antlers, and ivory.

This tiny mammoth-ivory carving is called the Lady of Brassempouy after the place in France where it was found. It is thought to be about 25,000 years old.

30,000 years ago

The numbers of Neanderthal people fall as modern humans spread across Europe. Eventually, Neanderthals are found only in southern Spain.

28,000 years ago

In Gibraltar, a rocky headland attached to the southern tip of Spain, the last known colony of Neanderthals finally dies out.

20,000 years ago

The last glacial period is at its coldest. So much water is locked up in ice sheets covering North America, Europe, and Asia that sea levels are at least 200 feet lower than they are today. This exposes an area of land about 900 miles wide that today lies under the Bering Sea, between Siberia and Alaska.

Ice ages

Ice ages have occurred frequently throughout Earth's history. They are times when the climate cools down so much that ice caps form at the poles. During an ice age, the ice caps grow larger or smaller. They are large during a glacial period. They are smaller during an interglacial period. Today, we could be living in an interglacial period of the last ice age. The ice caps at the poles today are small compared to those at other times. During the last glacial period, ice covered much of Europe, Asia, and North America.

Scientists still debate about what causes ice ages. They are probably due to many factors, including changes in Earth's orbit around the Sun and the chemicals in the atmosphere.

The white areas show the extent of polar ice caps 20,000 years ago, during the last glacial period.

Cave paintings

Stone Age cave paintings have been found in many caves in Europe. They were painted between 35,000 and 18,000 years ago by modern humans called Cro-Magnons. They

are named after the place in France where they lived. The paintings are often very realistic. They depict mainly large wild animals, such as bison, horses, woolly mammoths, deer, and lions. The images were drawn with paint made from powdered rocks and minerals. Sometimes the outline of the animal was cut into the rock first. We cannot be sure exactly why people made these paintings. They may have been "hunting magic," intended to increase the number of animals to hunt, or simply to record events.

12,000 years ago

Modern humans cross the Bering "land bridge" from Siberia into Alaska. They were following the animals they hunted, such as reindeer and mammoths. From there they spread southward until they reached the farthest tip of South America.

Possible routes modern humans took as they crossed from Asia into North America. From there they went to South America.

11,000 years ago

The last glacial period comes to an end. The Earth's climate warms up once again. The ice caps melt and sea levels rise. Land once covered in ice starts to recover. New plants grow, especially trees. Animals, such as bison, horses, and reindeer move into these new areas, followed closely by human hunters.

10,000 years ago

Animals that had thrived in the cold tundra during the last freezing period start to become extinct. The woolly rhinoceros, cave lion, and *Megaloceros* all die out at this time. Woolly mammoths survive only in very remote areas of northern Siberia.

4000 years ago

In Siberia, the woolly mammoth becomes extinct.

The woolly mammoth, one of the last survivors of the Ice Age.

Glossary

bog An area of wet, spongy ground.

burin A sharp, pointed tool made of flint.

clan A group of people, like a large family, with common ancestors.

dung Animal waste.

flint Hard, dark quartz that makes a spark when struck. It is used to start fires.

kindling Easily burnable material used for starting a fire.

matriarch An older female who leads the group.

migration Seasonal journey to find food and warmer weather.

pigment Material that gives color to paint or other substances.

scavenge To gather food or materials left behind from animals, storms, or other natural processes.

shaman A spiritual leader who is believed to be able to speak with spirits and use other forms of magic to cure illness or control events.

tepee A cone-shaped tent usually made of animal skins

tundra A flat, treeless plain in arctic regions where the lower layers of soil are always frozen.

Further Reading

Books

DK Publishing. *Early Humans*. New York: DK Children, 2005.

Harrison, David L. *Cave Detectives: Unraveling the Mystery of an Ice Age Cave*. San Francisco: Chronicle Books, 2007.

Internet Sites

Prehistoric Humans
http://www.kidspast.com/world-history/0001-prehistoric-humans.php

Virtually the Ice Age
http://www.creswell-crags.org.uk/virtuallytheiceage/

Welcome to the Stone Ages
http://museums.ncl.ac.uk/flint/menu.html

Index